Aristolochia littoralis

Nymphaea variata

For Ricardo, Gabriel, and Dylan~
may you never lose your Brookline wonder.

And for my father, Raymond Yee,
who inspired my love for tidepools and butterflies.

For further information, contact:
Tumblehome, Inc.
201 Newbury St, Suite 201
Boston, MA 02116
https://tumblehomebooks.org/

Library of Congress Control Number: 2024939956
ISBN 13: 978-1-943431-84-7
ISBN 10: 1-943431-84-1

Yee, Tammy / Glass Wonders / Tammy Yee — 1st ed
Book and illustrations by Tammy Yee

Printed in Taiwan
10 9 8 7 6 5 4 3 2 1

Glass Wonders

The Story of
Leopold and Rudolf Blaschka

By Tammy Yee

Leopold leaned over the rail. The ship sat motionless
on the glassy sea.

He threw a coin overboard.

The ocean erupted into a thousand flashes of
light, mirrored by the starry sky
above.

*"An indescribably beautiful scene originates...
it is as if they wanted to lure the enchanted
observer into a realm of fairies."*

~ Leopold Blaschka

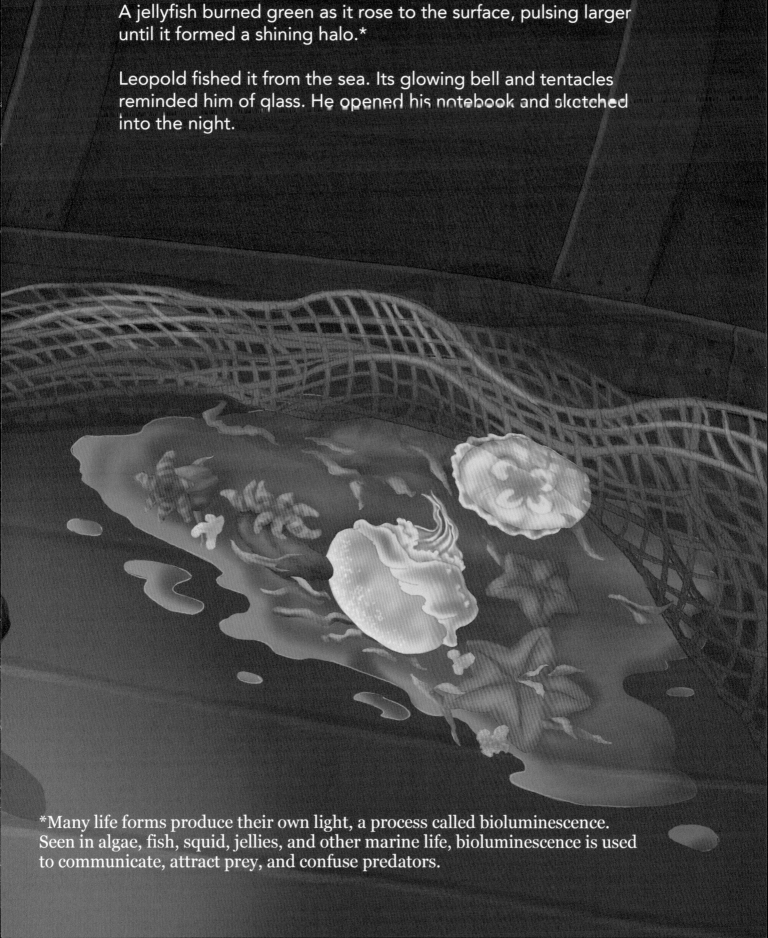

A jellyfish burned green as it rose to the surface, pulsing larger until it formed a shining halo.*

Leopold fished it from the sea. Its glowing bell and tentacles reminded him of glass. He opened his notebook and sketched into the night.

*Many life forms produce their own light, a process called bioluminescence. Seen in algae, fish, squid, jellies, and other marine life, bioluminescence is used to communicate, attract prey, and confuse predators.

Back in his studio, Leopold pushed aside his work: brooches adorned with forget-me-nots, flasks for laboratories, and glass eyes in all colors and sizes.

His voyage had reignited an inner flame. He had always enjoyed sketching nature. Now he wondered, *could he also sketch in glass?*

He stooped over his lampworking table. Air whooshed through leather bellows, stoking the flame into a thin blue torch.

He pulled and spun the molten glass with tongs and tweezers, until out of the fire emerged...

A stem. A leaf.

A flower.

Leopold held his creation up to the window. It was as if he was sculpting in light.

"One cannot hurry glass. It will take its own time. If we try to hasten it beyond its limits, it resists and no longer obeys us. We have to humor it."

~ Leopold Blaschka

Word of Leopold's glass bouquets reached a Czech prince.

Prince Camille de Rohan invited Leopold to his castle. He led Leopold through his greenhouse where sprays of orchids shimmered like butterflies and asked, *could Leopold create plants that would never wilt?*

Leopold was astonished! His glass flowers were a hobby that he never imagined were worthy of a prince. Still, he agreed to try.

Over the next two years, he crafted nearly a hundred glass plants.

The delighted prince mounted Leopold's creations on tree trunks in his palace.

Some of Leopold's sculptures were displayed in a museum's garden pavilion in Dresden, Germany.

Professor Ludwig Reichenbach marveled at their brilliance. As the museum director, he was responsible for preserving specimens for scientists to study. However, sea anemones and other soft-bodied creatures lost their shape and color over time.

The professor wondered, *could Leopold fashion sea anemones that would never fade?*

Leopold was puzzled. How could he make models of animals that he had never seen?

But he had seen such animals! He found the sketches he had made aboard his ocean voyage, and pulled a book from his shelf. Anemones bloomed like wildflowers from the pages.

Leopold fired up his lamp. He mixed enamels and colored glass. He dipped copper wire into molten glass so that dazzling beads formed like dew. Out of the fire emerged…

A column. A disk. Tentacles.

Soon he was creating models for museums and universities around the world. Customers ordered from Leopold's catalog of more than 600 kinds of brittle stars, sea cucumbers, and jellyfish for $0.30 to $6.50 each!

CATALOGUE
— of —
GLASS MODELS
— of —
Invertebrate Animals

Leopold Blaschka

Leopold's son, Rudolf, helped his father as best he could. He swept the floor, fed coals to the stove, and sorted glass and ground pigments.

At age 13 he learned lampworking from his father...

...and six years later he joined the family business.

"Many people think that we have some
secret apparatus by which we can squeeze
glass suddenly into these forms, but it is
not so. We have tact. My son Rudolf
has more than I have, because he is
my son, and tact increases in every
generation."

~ Leopold Blaschka

A

YEAR at the SHORE

BY

PHILIP HENRY GOSSE

WITH THIRTY-SIX ILLUSTRATIONS BY THE AUTHOR

LONDON
1865

The Blaschkas studied books about sealife. But the illustrations were flat, and didn't show the true shapes of the animals.

Bunodes gemmacea

They studied preserved specimens. But the specimens were dull, and didn't show the animals' true colors.

So they ordered living creatures from Italy, England, and the Baltic Sea, and kept them in aquariums. Anemones and snails arrived wrapped in seaweed and packed in jars.

Rudolf traveled to the coast of the Adriatic Sea to sketch his marine subjects firsthand.

The Blaschkas used their jewelry-making skills to craft fine details.

Octopuses' heads and tentacles were blown from glass tubes. Paint, cotton fibers, and gelatin added color, texture, and strength. Suckers were sorted in matchboxes, then pasted like gems along each tentacle.

Real shells adorned glass snails.

Delicate plankton, graceful sea slugs,
and billowing jellyfish filled the studio.

One day a visitor arrived from Boston, Massachusetts. Professor George Lincoln Goodale was the director of Harvard's Botanical Museum, and he was unhappy with the dried plants that were used to teach students. He had seen the Blaschkas' glasswork and he came to ask, *could they create models that looked like living plants?*

Making marine models was a successful business. Why should Leopold and Rudolf return to making plants? However, they agreed to make a few samples.

The models were shipped to Boston, but arrived in pieces. Goodale could only imagine what the undamaged sculptures had looked like! He asked a wealthy former student, Mary Ware, and her mother Elizabeth if they would sponsor a collection of glass flowers for Harvard.

Yes, they would!

Harvard offered the Blaschkas a 10-year contract so they could devote themselves entirely to plants. Their models became more and more detailed, with every root, leaf, flower, and seed in its proper place.

Leopold studied shrubs and trees that he grew from seeds and cuttings sent by Harvard.

Rudolf journeyed to Jamaica and throughout the United States, making hundreds of sketches.

He was traveling when
he learned of his father's passing.
He hurried home.

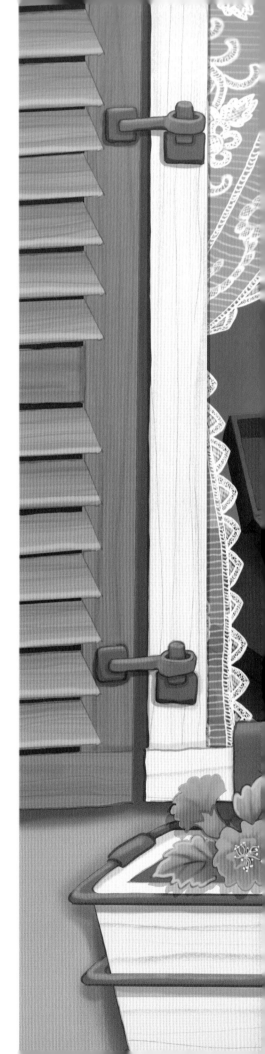

The studio seemed empty without Leopold, yet Rudolf felt his presence: in Leopold's sunlit garden, in the silent bellows of his worktable, and in his unfinished flowers. Rudolf wondered, *could he continue without his father by his side?*

He sat in Leopold's chair and took a deep breath.

Yes. Yes, he could.

The lamp whooshed to life. Glass stems sprouted luminous buds. Bees gathered nectar and pollen from yellow blossoms. And mold bloomed on rotting fruit.

Rudolf had no children, so there was no one to whom he could teach the family business. Eventually, the Blaschkas' lampworking secrets were lost.

"I was daunted to see what seemed a little old man, legs that were not strong, very rounded, stooped shoulders, and an exceedingly white face... It all leaves you breathless that anyone can and will do such work."

~ Mary Ware, describing her visit with Rudolf

The Ware Collection of Glass Flowers has remained in pristine condition through the years.

"[An] iron staircase leads to the Ware Collection of Blaschka Glass Models... With delight and emotion, I saw all the old friends united here, and I can report to you with joy that everything, even the oldest things, are still nice in form and color, just as we delivered them."

~ Rudolf Blaschka, visiting the collection on his trip to the United States

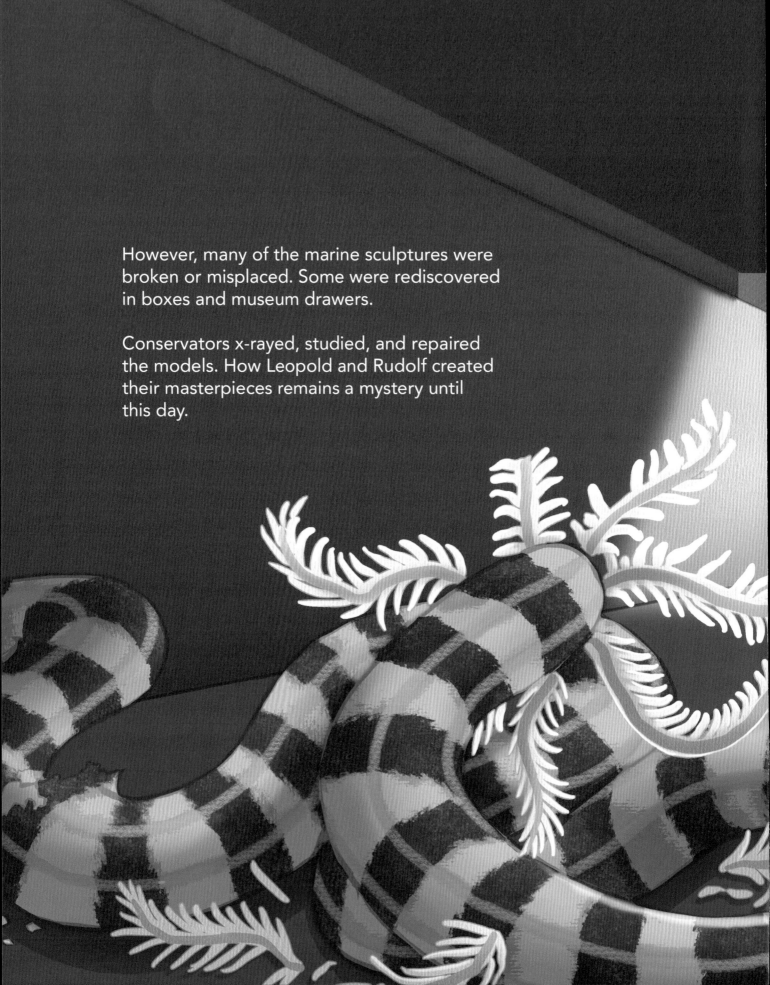

However, many of the marine sculptures were broken or misplaced. Some were rediscovered in boxes and museum drawers.

Conservators x-rayed, studied, and repaired the models. How Leopold and Rudolf created their masterpieces remains a mystery until this day.

Inspired by an ocean voyage more than 150 years ago, Rudolf and Leopold did what they loved best: recreating nature in art.

Their genius lives on in their glass wonders.

TIMELINE

1822 Leopold is born on May 27 in Böhmisch-Aicha (now in the Czech Republic) to Josef and Franciska Blaschka, joining a family of glassworkers.

1846 Leopold marries Carolina Zimmerman. Together they have a son, Josef.

1850 Leopold's wife and son die of cholera. Grief-stricken, he is advised by his doctor to find comfort sketching plants in the countryside.

1852 Father, Josef, dies.

1853 Leopold seeks solace on an ocean voyage to the United States and is mesmerized by the jellyfish and invertebrates* he encounters.

1854 Leopold marries Carolina Reigel and opens a studio, crafting jewelry, glass eyes, and laboratory equipment. He makes glass flowers for amusement.

1857 Rudolf is born on June 17.

1860- 1862 Prince Camille de Rohan commissions glass plants. Leopold makes nearly 100 models for the prince's castle.

1863 Professor Ludwig Reichenbach commissions 12 sea anemone models.

1870 Rudolf assists his father in the studio and learns lampworking.

1876 Rudolf officially joins the family business.

1880s The Blaschkas collect living sea creatures in aquariums, and creating marine models for learning institutions becomes their primary business.

1886 Professor George Lincoln Goodale commissions samples of glass plants and secures funding from Mary and Elizabeth Ware.

1890 The Blaschkas sign an exclusive 10-year contract to create botanical models for Harvard.

1892 Rudolf travels to the United States and Jamaica, and visits the glass flowers at Harvard.

1895 Leopold dies on July 3. Rudolf returns home.

> *"In his delirium, [Leopold's] intention was to go to New York because there it would be much nicer than Hosterwitz, his Rudolf would be with him, and he could work together with him."*
> ~Carolina Blaschka, writing of Leopold's death

1911 Rudolf marries Frieda Richter.

> *"We took a four day wedding trip to visit the Ore mountains and the...200 year old glass factory where my great-grandfather was master about 130-150 years ago."* ~Rudolf Blaschka

1923 Rudolf's mother, Carolina, dies.

1939 Rudolf dies on May 1, leaving unfinished projects on his worktable.

* Soft-bodied animals lacking a spine.

SOURCES

"Biographical Note: Leopold Blaschka." *The Archives of Rudolf and Leopold Blaschka and the Ware Collection of Blaschka Glass Models of Plants, 1886-2020: A Guide,* Botany Libraries, Economic Botany Library of Oakes Ames, Harvard University, p. 5.

"Biographical Note: Rudolf Blaschka." *The Archives of Rudolf and Leopold Blaschka and the Ware Collection of Blaschka Glass Models of Plants, 1886-2020: A Guide,* Botany Libraries, Economic Botany Library of Oakes Ames, Harvard University, pp 5-6.

Brill, Elizabeth R., et al. *Sea Creatures in Glass: The Blaschka Marine Animals at Harvard.* Scala Arts & Heritage, 2016.

Harvell, Drew. *Sea of Glass: Searching for the Blaschkas' Fragile Legacy in an Ocean at Risk.* University of California Press, 2019.

Reiling, Henri. *The Blaschkas' Glass Animal Models: Origins of Design.* Journal of Glass Studies, Vol. 40, 1998, pp 105-126. Corning Museum of Glass. www.jstor.org/stable/i24184895

Rossi-Wilcox, Susan M, and David Whitehouse. "Blaschkas' Glass Models of Invertebrate Animals (1863-1890)." All About Glass | Corning Museum of Glass, 2011, www.cmog.org/article/blaschkas-glass-models-invertebrate-animals-1863-1890.

Schultes, Richard Evans, et al. *The Glass Flowers at Harvard.* Botanical Museum of Harvard University, 2004.

ABOUT THE AUTHOR

Tammy Yee grew up in Honolulu, Hawaii, where she explored tide pools, caught crayfish in island streams, raised butterflies, and dreamed of someday merging her interests in art and science. She learned of the Ware Collection of Blaschka Glass Models of Plants while living in Brookline with her husband and two young sons. However, it was the discovery of the bond between a father and son that inspired her to write this story.

Her most recent biography is *The Angel of Santo Tomas: The Story of Fe del Mundo.*